CW01667814

The Battle of Barnet.

Frederick Cass

The Battle of Barnet.

Cass, Frederick
British Library, Historical Print Editions
British Library
1885?
52 p. ; 8º.

The BiblioLife Network

This project was made possible in part by the BiblioLife Network (BLN), a project aimed at addressing some of the huge challenges facing book preservationists around the world. The BLN includes libraries, library networks, archives, subject matter experts, online communities and library service providers. We believe every book ever published should be available as a high-quality print reproduction; printed on- demand anywhere in the world. This insures the ongoing accessibility of the content and helps generate sustainable revenue for the libraries and organizations that work to preserve these important materials.

The following book is in the "public domain" and represents an authentic reproduction of the text as printed by the original publisher. While we have attempted to accurately maintain the integrity of the original work, there are sometimes problems with the original book or micro-film from which the books were digitized. This can result in minor errors in reproduction. Possible imperfections include missing and blurred pages, poor pictures, markings and other reproduction issues beyond our control. Because this work is culturally important, we have made it available as part of our commitment to protecting, preserving, and promoting the world's literature.

GUIDE TO FOLD-OUTS, MAPS and OVERSIZED IMAGES

In an online database, page images do not need to conform to the size restrictions found in a printed book. When converting these images back into a printed bound book, the page sizes are standardized in ways that maintain the detail of the original. For large images, such as fold-out maps, the original page image is split into two or more pages.

Guidelines used to determine the split of oversize pages:

- Some images are split vertically; large images require vertical and horizontal splits.
- For horizontal splits, the content is split left to right.
- For vertical splits, the content is split from top to bottom.
- For both vertical and horizontal splits, the image is processed from top left to bottom right.

THE BATTLE OF BARNET,

BY

FREDERICK CHARLES CASS, M.A.
of Balliol College, Oxford, Rector of Monken Hadley.

"I will away towards Barnet presently."
Hen. VI. iii. act v. sc. 1.

It is almost a truism to observe that whatever attraction in the present attaches to the place we inhabit is heightened by an interest derived from past associations. This is no more than to say that, as we gaze around us, we love to reproduce in fancy everything of moment that the scene we are contemplating has witnessed in bygone times. Pilgrims to the field of Waterloo will never be wanting, and, did not distance and want of communication interpose obstacles, there would be many found ready to gratify their eyes with a sight of the valley where the six hundred rode at Balaclava.

The troubled period of early English history commonly identified with the Wars of the Roses has always exercised a peculiar fascination over the mind of the student, and one of its most important episodes, if not the most decisive of all, was the great battle fought on Easter Day, 14 April 1471, in the immediate neighbourhood of Barnet. It has been said that the fifteenth century was not remarkable for its great men, that few leading spirits passed across the stage to leave their individual impression on succeeding generations, and the assertion may not perhaps, up to a certain point, be destitute of truth. An eminent modern writer has pronounced it a degraded age, and has gone so far as to argue that "the vulgar neatness and deceptive regularity"* of its very penmanship are suggestive of decadence. But if undistinguished by any marked personality in the characters which it produced, it was at least an era in which secret forces were at work to prepare for and shape a vast social and religious revolution that was to come. Education was extending, and the interesting Paston correspondence may be taken as a proof that ability to write was growing common.† The Pastons were a wealthy and respectable family in Norfolk, which indicates that a rank below the highest aristocracy was participating in the movement of the age. National and domestic life, considered apart from the events which historians have mostly seized upon, were becoming gradually moulded into, and insensibly drawing towards, the form which they were to bear afterwards. French and Latin, as official languages, were giving place by degrees to English, and the change grew more and more conspicuous when the loss of her French provinces led to a complete separation of this country from France. Men's wills about this time

* Canon Stubbs; Constitutional Hist. of England. See art. in Edin. Review July 1879.

† This collection contains a letter, dated 23 Feb. 1478/9 from William Paston, junr. then a scholar at Eton. Eton and King's College Cambridge were founded by Henry VI. about 1440—1. Hallam, Lit. of Europe, i. 168, 169. Middle Ages iii. 597. Fenn's Paston Letters, *Letter 405*.

began to be transcribed in the mother tongue. Wealthy citizens and their wives, as their testamentary dispositions prove, amassed plate and jewellery, furs, and rich robes. Towards the close of the century they were possessed of a few printed books. But during that interval of civil strife and bloodshed busy brains were agitating in secret the questions that were to strive after an open solution at a later day. The dawn might be lurid and tempestuous, but a bright morning was to follow. Art and letters, which for centuries had vegetated with sickly growth in monastic seclusion, had reached the limits beyond which no further development was possible, except under changed conditions. The change had at last come, and already they were ripening into the vital energy that should inspire them with vigour to blossom into newness of life. The following century was the age of the so-called Renaissance, the age of the great Italian painters, of Leo X., of the Medici at Florence, of the Reformation, of the Elizabethan statesmen and discoverers. In 1471, the year of the battle of Barnet, William Caxton set up a printing press at Bruges.* In 1483 Martin Luther was born. In 1492 Columbus discovered America. In 1497 Vasco de Gama doubled the Cape of Good Hope and opened a new path to India.

Not to travel too far beyond the limits of this island, it is noteworthy that, whilst the rivalry of the royal houses in England had well nigh extinguished the old

* He came to England, as is supposed, in 1476, and the first book printed in England, though not the first English book that he printed, was produced in 1477.

nobility, preparing the way to its later and easy subjugation under the Tudors, and the uprising of a new aristocracy, recruited largely from the ranks of commerce, in France Louis XI. was silently occupied, with spider-like ingenuity, in consolidating the monarchy by bringing the great fiefs of the crown within his control. A like result was consequently in course of accomplishment at the same time, though by different agencies, in the two neighbouring nations. Henry VII. and Charles VIII., on ascending their respective thrones, found a stage cleared for them, the one through violence and the other by statecraft. In religion the storm was already gathering, which, in the succeeding generation, burst at the invocation of Luther and shook the spiritual supremacy of Rome to its base. Wycliffe had come and gone. Lollardy, as it was called, was rife in the land as early as the reigns of Henry IV and Henry V. if not before. In the year 1427 one William Redhed of Barnet, a maltman, being suspected of it, renounced his heresy. Report went that he had become infected by the pernicious doctrines of the then rector of Totteridge.

The annalists of the period were possessed of such scanty sources of information, and have handed down to us statements so conflicting, and so coloured with partisan bias, that the events chronicled, if we confined ourselves to these, would restrict us within the limits of a very meagre and unsatisfactory narrative. To form a correct estimate, however, of the value of any historical fact, one must be acquainted with the incidents preceding, contemporary, and subsequent, and this applies not only to history on a large scale,—

the history, that is, of a nation, of an epoch, of a political convulsion, in other words, of a revolution,—but to every detail of history, to every episode of history. A French historian has lately written that "pour avoir une notion juste de l'État, de la religion, du droit, de la richesse, il faut être au préalable historien, jurisconsulte, économiste, avoir recueilli des myriades de faits et posséder, outre une vaste érudition, une finesse très-exerçée et toute spéciale."* In the present instance, accordingly, disavowing all pretension to any of these qualifications, it will be well to run through some of the leading historical events that preceded and led up to the great battle. To do this we must go back three-quarters of a century, to the commencement of that dynastic change which occasioned so much subsequent unsettlement in the succession to the English throne.

After the deposition of Richard II in 1399 and the usurpation of his cousin the crown was a subject of contention, until the overthrow of Richard III at Bosworth, in 1485, placed it, for upwards of a century, on the head of the Tudors. In 1377 Edward III, having outlived his early fame, had closed a long reign of fifty years and was succeeded by his grandson Richard II, the only child of the Black Prince, who died in his father's lifetime. The well-known John of Gaunt, duke of Lancaster, father of Henry IV,—"old John of Gaunt, time-honour'd Lancaster,"—had been a personage of considerable importance in the kingdom during the minority of his nephew, but had failed to

* H. Taine, l'Ancien Régime, p. 239.

achieve popularity. He was the third, but eldest surviving, son of Edward III at the date of his father's death. An elder brother, Lionel, duke of Clarence, the second son of Edward, had, however, left a daughter Philippa, who married Edmund Mortimer, earl of March. Roger Mortimer, earl of March, their son, killed by the rebels in Ireland in 1399, the year of Richard's dethronement, was the legitimate representative of the Plantagenets, in the event of Richard's decease without issue. He left a son Edmund, his successor in the earldom, and a daughter Anne Mortimer, who, upon her brother's death issueless, became the heiress of the house of Clarence.

There remained a yet younger son of Edward, named Edmund, styled of Langley from his birth-place at King's Langley in Hertfordshire, where he lies buried, and where his tomb in the church has been recently restored and a stained window presented by the Queen to commemorate the royal connection with the village. This prince, previously earl of Cambridge, was raised to the dukedom of York. Richard, earl of Cambridge, his son, beheaded in 1415, married that Anne Mortimer, of whom mention has just been made as the heiress of the house of Clarence, and from this alliance was born Richard duke of York, father of Edward IV. It is necessary to keep this connection in view, as it was afterwards made the foundation of the Yorkist claim to the crown. The descendant of Lionel duke of Clarence was the direct heiress, and the representative of the younger, or Yorkist, branch, by his intermarriage with that heiress, pretended to a joint inheritance of her title.

By combining astuteness with sagacity Henry IV succeeded in keeping what he had acquired, though with reason enough for the conclusion that "uneasy lies the head that wears a crown." The parting injunction delivered to his son, that he should not suffer his dominions to remain at peace, but keep his turbulent subjects, especially the barons, always employed in foreign war, furnishes the key to his policy. Usurper that he was, he gladly obtained a parliamentary sanction to his elevation, and thereby hoped to supply the defect of hereditary right. In the hour of his accession he was the popular idol.

——" All tongues cried—God save thee, Bolingbroke!
You would have thought the very windows spake,
So many greedy looks of young and old
Through casements darted their desiring eyes
Upon his visage." *

His brilliant successor, grace to his achievements in France and the crowning victory of Agincourt, was, at the time of his premature death, firmly seated upon the throne both by parliamentary sanction and the predominance of individual character. The royal authority, as distinct from personal influence, was weak notwithstanding. A taint of usurpation still rested upon it, and his cousin, the earl of Cambridge, had been executed in 1415, on a charge of conspiracy against him.

The position and prospects of the feeble infant, Henry VI, not yet a year old, whom he left behind him, were more precarious. John duke of Bedford

* Rich. II. act v. sc. 2.

and Humphry duke of Gloucester, the two brothers of Henry V, were in their way remarkable men,—the one distinguished for his statesmanlike qualities and the other one of the earliest promoters of learning,—but the former was removed by death in 1435, and the latter was of too unstable and self-seeking a disposition to guide the national destinies. His place of burial in St. Alban's abbey is well known, and he bequeathed a library,* valuable for the time, to the university of Oxford. Amongst those who came under his patronage were Lydgate the poet and John of Whethamstede, the versifying abbot of St. Alban's, who composed the inscription on Thomas Frowyke within the tower of South Mimms church.

As Henry advanced to manhood, a natural weakness of character was redeemed by personal blamelessness, by upright principles, by a love of everything that was pure and true, by the patronage of letters, and by a conscientious desire to promote the happiness and welfare of his people. These qualities, added to the prestige of his father's exploits, no doubt went for something in securing his position for a time. The rapid extinction of the English power in France had caused the French nation to be regarded in a very hostile spirit, and the supposed ascendency of Margaret of Anjou's resolute character over her husband began to be dreaded. Normandy had been already wrested from England in 1450, Guienne in 1451, Bordeaux in 1453. Calais alone remained. The insanity of the King—an hereditary taint derived from

* Hallam, Lit. of Europe, i. 110. ii. 260.

his grandfather, Charles VI of France, eventually brought the rival parties in the state face to face. The influence of the Queen had been considerably augmented by the birth of a Prince of Wales in October 1453, whilst, about the same date, the King's malady visited him in an apparently hopeless form. It was expedient that the direction of affairs should be committed to a regent for the time that the royal incapacity lasted, and the popular inclination pointed to Richard duke of York, who has been described as "a prince of no mean capacity, distinguished for his bravery, but of an irresolute and feeble character, indiscreet, fickle, and obstinate by turns."* Hume says he "was a man of valour and abilities, of a prudent conduct and mild dispositions."† In February 1454 he was named Protector, but his authority terminated with the Christmas following, when the King regained possession of his faculties.

From this period Henry, though in the intervals of his disease able in some measure to reassert himself, was more or less an instrument in the hands of others. After his first recovery he allowed himself to be governed by the advice of the duke of Somerset, who had suffered imprisonment for supposed mismanagement of the English interests in France. The duke of York, with Richard Nevile earl of Salisbury and his more famous son Richard earl of Warwick, withdrew to the north, and the civil war soon afterwards began with the first battle of St. Alban's, fought on the 22 of

* Lord Brougham, England and France under the House of Lancaster, p. 319.

† Vol. iv. 52. ed. of 1793.

May 1455, when Somerset was killed and King Henry wounded in the neck with an arrow. With varying fortune the struggle continued during the ensuing years. Pretentious reconciliations that bore no fruit and shifting party combinations followed, but it speedily became apparent that the nation, broadly considered, was divided at this time between the party of the Queen and the party of the duke of York, and that the question must be left to the sword to decide. It would demand more space than we can afford were it attempted, however briefly, to run through all the leading incidents of this fratricidal strife. At length, in 1460, the earl of March, who now comes prominently to the front, and who is better known as Edward IV, eldest son of the duke of York, crossed from Ireland with the earls of Salisbury * and Warwick. King Henry was shortly afterwards taken prisoner at Northampton, and the duke of York not only reassumed his functions as Protector but asserted a claim to the throne itself as rightful heir. A compromise was effected between the parties, by which it was stipulated and agreed that Henry should enjoy the crown for his life, but that the duke and his heirs should succeed him.

Margaret of Anjou was not one to acquiesce tamely in such a renunciation of her son's birthright, and at the sanguinary battle of Wakefield her forces defeated those of the duke of York, and he himself was slain. The story is well known how the overbearing woman

* Lord Salisbury was the son of Ralph Nevile, earl of Westmoreland. His sister had married Richard duke of York.

in the full flush of victory caused a paper crown to be affixed in mockery to her dead adversary's head, which was afterwards exposed upon the wall of York beside that of lord Salisbury, taken prisoner and decapitated at the same time.

The young earl of March became at once the inheritor of his father's pretensions. Upon his unopposed entrance into London after a second engagement at St. Alban's, in which, notwithstanding, the Lancastrians had the advantage, in February 1461, he was declared King, and Henry solemnly deposed. The years of the reign of Edward IV are reckoned from this time.

We must hurry past the terrible slaughter of Towton, where the hopes of the Red Rose underwent an utter overthrow, with all the stormy incidents of the next ten years, during which Edward's throne was assailed from time to time by the partisans of the Lancastrian cause, and come to the events which immediately conducted to the engagement with which we are concerned at this moment. At the accession of Edward, Margaret and her son escaped to the Continent, whilst her consort, after an interval of wandering and concealment, became a prisoner in the Tower as soon as the battle of Hexham was lost in 1464.

A word must now be said concerning the two leading characters, who from this time occupy the centre of the picture, and whose antagonism came to a close on Barnet field.

Edward, who was only nineteen years of age at the time of his elevation to the throne, was tall of stature, singularly handsome, winning in manners. pleasure-loving and self-indulgent, but, beneath this fascinating exterior, calculating, crafty, fearless, dissolute, cruel, and vindictive. That was not an age in which the gentler qualities of human nature had much scope for development in public men. He knew neither forbearance nor pity where there was an end to compass, and, being possessed of abilities above the average, was restrained by no scruple as to their employment. Like his contemporary Louis XI, his policy guided him towards the acquisition of absolute power, and with the citizens and their wives, a class now rising into new importance through the extinction of the old nobility, he achieved an immense popularity. The story is told of him that, when he asked a rich old lady for ten pounds towards a war with France, she answered, "For thy comely face thou shalt have twenty." The King thanked and kissed her, and the old woman made the twenty forty.*

Richard Nevile, earl of Warwick, commonly known as the *King-maker*, Edward's powerful supporter at the beginning, though afterwards his most formidable adversary, owned vast possessions,† besides holding the important post of governor of Calais. No other nobleman could summon so many vassals and retainers into the field. It is said that, when he came to London, six oxen were consumed at a breakfast at Warwick's Inn in Holborn. He was in short a splendid outcome of feudalism and, being already the eldest son of the earl

* Green, Hist. of the English People, ii. 27.

† Philippe de Comines says that he received 80,000 crowns a year from appointments, in addition to his private property (son patrimoine).

of Salisbury, by a marriage with the heiress of the Beauchamps had acquired the Warwick title and estates. His character has been variously estimated. Hume insists upon his lavish hospitality and the magnificence of his tastes. The Burgundian chronicler,* a contemporary personally acquainted with the leading characters of his day, accuses him of double-dealing,—"tels ouvrages ne se sçavoient passer sans dissimulation."† We are perhaps justified in conceiving him to have been an able general and far-seeing politician, though at the same time greedy of wealth, jealous of power, and unscrupulous in the choice of means to secure either. Under conditions in which right is ever with the strongest, generosity and the other more humane qualities are not apt to be much considered. Warwick must be judged of according to the standard of his day, and by no severer test. To him Edward in a great measure owed his throne and, in return, honours had been showered upon the house of Nevile without stint. His brother, lord Montagu, in requital of the victory of Hexham, had been created earl of Northumberland, and endowed with the forfeited lands of the Percies. Another brother, George, was made archbishop of York and Chancellor.

The marriage of Edward with the fair widow,‡ Elizabeth Wydevile, in 1464, effected an unavoidable change in the relations hitherto subsisting between him and Warwick. The policy of the latter had lain in

* Philippe de Comines.

† A French commentator explains this word by *fourberie*.

‡ Her first husband, Sir John Grey, had fallen, on the Lancastrian side, in the second battle of St. Alban's.

the direction of a foreign alliance, as some equivalent for the loss of the French provinces. With a statesman's intuition he perceived that, in promoting a good understanding between Edward and Louis, opposed as the two men were by nature, he should best checkmate the hostility of Margaret. So long as Margaret of Anjou, a French princess, could look for French assistance, there was no likelihood of the house of York remaining securely seated on the English throne. But, when the King married a subject, the hopes based upon this policy totally failed. Besides which, the Wydevile family aimed at making themselves a power in the state, and were eager for the acquisition of rewards and dignities. At length an animosity which had long smouldered broke out into a flame. In 1469 the government fell absolutely into Warwick's hands, the King became his prisoner, and the ascendency of the Wydeviles received a check. Early in the following year the position of parties was once more reversed. This time it was Warwick's turn to flee and seek refuge abroad, but he had the King's younger brother, the duke of Clarence, in his company, and there can be little doubt but what the intention was to depose Edward and make Clarence, who had married Warwick's daughter Isabel, king in his brother's stead.

The result of Warwick's flight was a reconciliation with Margaret, through the intervention of the French King, who saw thereby a means of strengthening himself against the duke of Burgundy, and on the 13 Sep. 1470 the earl and Clarence, with Pembroke *

* Jasper Tudor, son of Sir Owen Tudor by Katharine of Valois, widow of Henry V.

and Oxford, sailing from Harfleur, landed at Dartmouth, issued proclamations in the name of Henry,* and marched straightway towards the north, where Edward was engaged in quelling an insurrection. He had relied much on the support of Montagu, Warwick's brother, whom he had created Marquis,—a profitless dignity,—in lieu of the earldom of Northumberland and its lands, restored to the Percies. Montagu had cherished ever since a secret hope of revenge, and his soldiers, to Edward's dismay, now raised the cry of 'Long live King Henry.' The Yorkist king perceived that there was not an instant to lose. Riding through the night, accompanied by 800 men, from Yorkshire to King's Lynn in Norfolk, crossing the Wash at some risk and with the loss of certain of his company,† he embarked with his followers on the 3rd of October in a few trading vessels for Alkmaar in Holland, where he threw himself on the protection of Charles duke of Burgundy, who had married his sister, Margaret of York. Shortly before her husband's flight, on the night of Oct. 1, the Queen had secretly stolen out of the Tower and gone by water to sanctuary at Westminster,‡ where a little later she gave birth to a son, afterwards the unfortunate Edward V. On Monday 22 October the unhappy Henry VI was removed from the lodging, which he had previously occupied, and transferred to

* Fabyan's Chronicle, ed. 1559.

† Fabyan.

‡ Stow, ed. 1615. Fabyan says that she rode into Westminster, and there registered herself for a sanctuary woman, with many other of Edward's friends.

the royal quarters in the Tower, but, upon the arrival of Clarence with lord Warwick and others on the Saturday following, he was conducted with all honour to the bishop's palace at St. Paul's.* There would seem, however, to have been no hesitation as to his incapacity to govern, and, though acknowledged once more as King,† Clarence and Warwick were appointed joint protectors of the realm during the minority of the young Edward, Prince of Wales, Henry's son.

Charles of Burgundy at first gave his guest a cold welcome, not willing to precipitate a rupture with Louis XI, and despatched the Lancastrian dukes of Somerset and Exeter, who since Towton had resided at his court, to Paris, to assure Margaret of his neutrality. By-and-by, apprehending that in any contest with France the weight of England might be thrown into the scale against him, owing to the good understanding between Louis and the present heads of the Lancastrian party, he determined to render assistance to his brother-in-law.

We are now brought to the commencement of 1471. Lord Warwick, apprized in January of the Yorkist intentions, ordered Montagu to levy an army in the north, and on the 2 of March, furnished with money

* Fabyan.

† In evidence of the general acquiescence in the restored order of things may be adduced the wills of Philip de la Place and William Elmett, which respectively bear date the 8 and 26 March, 1470—1. The former was proved P. C. C. on 18 April, the Thursday after the battle of Barnet. Both of them are headed "the yere of our lord god 1470, and the yere from the begynnyng of the reign of King Henry the vj[th] xlix, and of the getyng ageyne of his royall power the first yere." Book Wattis 1. 2.

by the duke of Burgundy, by whose instrumentality ships had likewise been equipped for him at Terveer in Zealand, Edward set sail from Flushing. In sight of Cromer, on the Norfolk coast, he sent on shore to discover how the country was affected; but learning that considerable preparations had been made in that quarter by the earl of Oxford * to resist him, he steered northwards, and on the 14th landed at Ravenspur, at the estuary of the Humber, on the Holderness or northern shore, the site of which has disappeared in sandbanks. He had with him a force of 2000 men, including a small body of trained German soldiers, armed with hand-guns, then a new weapon in war.† It is noteworthy that Henry of Bolingbroke had disembarked at the same place, when on his way to dethrone Richard II, and, adopting a similar line of policy, Edward in the first instance pushed on to York, where he received admission on the plea that his only purpose was to claim its dukedom, his rightful inheritance.

Warwick, in the meantime, had been anxiously looking for Margaret's return to England. Since the previous November she had been on the opposite coast, awaiting a favourable wind for her passage,‡ but still the wind continued adverse and delayed her presence

* Oxford, who had estates at Wivenhoe in Essex, was strong in the eastern counties.

† Fleetwood says he landed with 500 men. This may, however, refer to the number of those who actually disembarked with himself. Fabyan makes the number "about 1000 in all," and calls the foreign soldiers *Flemings*

‡ Fabyan.

where, at such a crisis, it was most needed. On the 23 of February, a week before the departure of Edward's expedition, the duke of Exeter had come to London and, on the following day, Warwick rode through the city towards Dover in the hope of meeting the Queen. She came not, and after a time he returned to London, the progress of events requiring him elsewhere.*

To go back to Edward, who without delay set forward with his little army from York. As he went southwards numbers flocked to his standard. We have to bear in mind the conditions of military service under the feudal tenure, according to which every great lord led his own vassals and retainers into the field. So long, therefore, as the adhesion of any powerful noble remained in doubt, the expectations built upon his support could never fail to be a source of uneasiness. Upon the attitude of Clarence and Montagu everything now seemed to hinge, but as Edward approached Pontefract, Montagu, who lay there, made no sign. He may not even have been aware of the nearness of the invading force, which at this point diverged four miles from the straight road and thereby passed unobserved, resuming the direct way afterwards.† Fabyan says that by favour and fair words he passed him, since Montagu, who had a far superior force at command, might have arrested his progress, had he so willed it. At all events, on reaching Nottingham, being already, as is said, at the head of 4000 men and, whether by cajolery or stratagem,

* Fabyan.

† Grafton, ed. of 1569, p. 702.

having Montagu now well in his rear, Edward first openly threw off the mask and issued proclamations as King. From Nottingham, following the direct road, be advanced to Leicester and thence to Coventry, where Warwick, having hastened from the capital, was awaiting reinforcements under Clarence and Montagu. Here Edward offered him battle, which the earl declined, in uncertainty as to the course that might be adopted by either leader, and the result justified his apprehensions, for the arrival of Clarence —"false, fleeting, perjur'd Clarence"*—was immediately succeeded by a reconciliation with his brother and the junction of their forces. Warwick himself would perhaps have willingly evaded the gathering peril by a like treachery, had not the coming of the duke of Exeter and earl of Oxford, two staunch Lancastrians, compelled him to stand firm. It is almost impossible—the accounts are so conflicting—to arrive at any assured conclusion as to the relative strength of the opposing forces at this juncture. That of the earl may have been at this time inferior in numbers, and he may have still entertained doubts of his brother's fidelity. The approach of the latter notwithstanding drove Edward to a prompt decision, and it became the question of the hour which of the rival armies should first gain London. In this Edward was once more successful. Outmarching his adversary and passing through St. Alban's in his way, he appeared before the city gates on the 11 of April, being the Thursday before Easter. The occasion was critical. Any delay

* Richard III. act i. sc. 4.

or obstruction that gave time for the arrival of Warwick and his army might have reversed the posture of affairs.

King Henry and the archbishop of York, Warwick's brother, were at the bishop of London's palace, having ridden through the streets, at the rumour of Edward's approach, to urge the people to be true. The heart of the citizens was however with the Yorkist prince. The towns had as a rule espoused his cause. Thomas Urswyke, the recorder, with certain of the leading aldermen, having ordered the armed population, who were keeping the city "in harness," to go home to their dinners, Edward was by them admitted within the walls through a postern gate.* From this moment the city was won, and though the citizens were at first sharply rebuked for their desertion they were promptly retaken into favour. Edward's first act on entering London was to ride to St. Paul's, where he made an offering "at the rood of the north door,"† proceeding thence to the bishop of London's palace, where he found Henry almost alone. King Henry and the archbishop were consigned the same afternoon to the Tower, but it is open to question whether the latter had not connived at the whole proceeding.‡ Urswyke was knighted immediately, and on the following 22 May—the very day of Henry's death—

* Warkworth Chronicle, 15. 21 † Fabyan.

‡ Sir John Paston writes on the 18 April:—"My lord archbishop is in the Tower; nevertheless I trust to God that he shall do well enough: he hath a safeguard for him and me both; nevertheless we have been troubled since, but now I understand that he hath a pardon; and so we hope well."

raised to the dignity of Chief Baron of the Exchequer.*

Edward made no long stay in London. Warwick was in pursuit, and it was essential that his progress should be barred. Intelligence had been transmitted that he had advanced as far as Barnet † and the news overran the city like wildfire. Dividing his army into four parts, ‡ Edward sallied forth to meet his foe. Everything had been prepared effectually, even if hurriedly, as for a supreme effort. To the force which he had brought with him to London was joined a company of young, vigorous, and picked men, fully equipped with the newest weapons and engines of warfare that the age could furnish. His army was in short well found in every appliance that money, employed without stint, could procure. Accordingly, though he had only entered the city on Thursday, he rode out towards Barnet on Saturday afternoon, being Easter Eve, with the hapless Henry VI in his company, prepared, it may be, to turn the presence of his captive to account, should he himself be placed in jeopardy. On reaching Barnet, "ten small miles distant," as the old chronicler has it, his advanced guard drove out of the town some of lord Warwick's scouts and pursued them for more than half a mile, until, "by an hedge side," they found themselves face to face with a considerable body of the enemy.

We left Warwick at Coventry. His cause demanded expedition, and he resolved upon a vigorous pursuit of the enemy, in the hope that some detention, how-

* Foss, Judges, iv. 458.

† St. Alban's, according to Rapin, i. 613. ‡ Halle. Grafton.

ever slight, might impede his march and force him to accept battle before he could reach London. London, as Warwick was well persuaded, was incapable of defence, whilst its citizens, however affected at heart, would probably cast in their lot with the stronger party. Still he trusted that Edward might be kept outside the walls till he could come up with him.* But as he advanced the tidings of Edward's peaceful entry were brought to him, and he determined to stake everything upon the issue of one decisive engagement. With this purpose he halted at St. Alban's, as well to refresh his troops as to consider his plans. Thence he removed to Barnet, about ten miles distant from either place.† Not along the monotonously even road that now stretches between Barnet and the summit of Ridge hill, but by narrow devious tracks no longer frequented, along the irregular street of South Mimms village, over the high bridge at the Wash, which there are grounds for conceiving to have been already in existence,‡ past Dancer's hill § and Kick's end, the array of mounted knights, and stalwart archers and bill-men, and roystering condottieri, or free companies, ready to cut anybody's throat for hire, came thronging on, until Gladmore heath was occupied, then an open plain to the north of the little town of Barnet. There

* Rapin. † Grafton.

‡ Roger Wright, of Hadley, maltman, in his will, dated 2 May, 1502, leaves 20*s*. to the repair of the "high waye betwene hight brygge & the strete of Southmymmes." Hist. of the Parish of Monken Hadley, 132.

§ John Coningsby esq. in his will, dated 28 June 1543, speaks of his messuage and lands at "Daunsers hill in Southe-mymes."

can be no doubt as to the locality. Sir John Paston, who was engaged in the battle on the Lancastrian side, writing to his mother from sanctuary in London on the Thursday following, states it to have taken place half a mile from Barnet, which agrees exactly with the spot mentioned by Edward Halle, judge in the sheriff's court, and therefore a competent authority, who died in 1547, sufficiently near the date to have conversed in his lifetime with some who were present. "This toune" (Barnet), he says, "standeth on a hill, on whose toppe is a faire plain, for twoo armies to joyne together;" and on one part of this plain Warwick "pitched his field." Another annalist* employs the same expression, "halfe a mile from Barnet." The present Hadley green, with the level ground contiguous to it, exactly answers the description.

The position was well chosen, though we have to bear in mind the altered conditions of military science at the present day. A modern commander similarly circumstanced would doubtless have occupied the little town in force, entrenching himself along the high ground sloping towards the south-east between the top of Barnet hill and Hadley church, and placing his reserves somewhere to the west on Barnet common to secure his right flank from being turned. With his artillery he would have swept the ascent of Barnet hill and would have taken care to line the edge of Hadley wood with riflemen. It is worth any one's while to rest for a few moments at the eastern entrance of the town and study the fair prospect that lies at his

* Stow.

feet. Before all things let him bear in mind that the embankment carrying the high road, which is in a state of continual disintegration, was only constructed within living memory, and that the ancient roadway passed close to the Old Red Lion at the foot of the hill and the outlet of the Totteridge lane. He can hardly fail to observe that a ridge in his front, taking a south easterly direction, divides the prospect into two pleasant valleys, what may be termed a *mamelon*, of slight elevation, terminating this ridge just beyond the present railway station. The ridge in question, along which the road leaves Barnet in its course towards London, is a watershed from which the brooks on the one side find their way to the Lea and on the other to the Brent. An army posted at Barnet would, in consequence, have had a choice of three approaches to the capital, either by the valley of the Lea eastwards, or along the central ridge towards its northern suburbs, or by the Brent valley in the direction of the villages lying outside its walls to the west, as Charing, Kensington, &c. Of these three routes, in the event of any catastrophe befalling Edward's army, Warwick had the selection open to him.

On reaching Hadley green or Gladmore heath, as the locality appears to have been then designated, he had ample time before him for the choice of his ground. He was first in the field, by many hours at least. Any attempt to define the exact position which he adopted must be at best conjectural, but he was an experienced commander, and this reflection may come in aid of our conjectures.

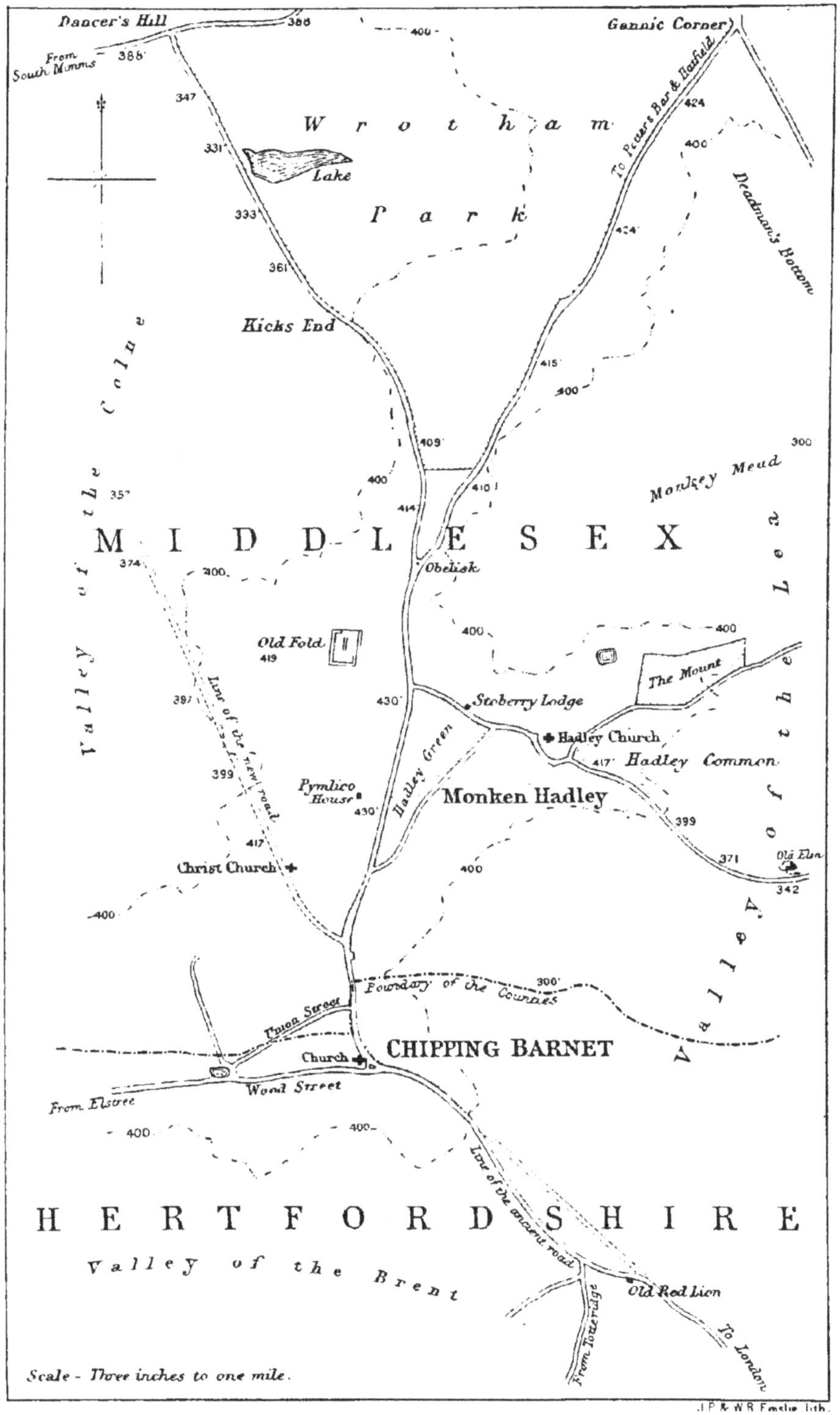

J.P. & W.R. Emslie lith.

A person taking his stand at Sir Jeffrey Sambrooke's obelisk, and looking southwards, will notice that the ground rises, with a scarcely perceptible ascent in front, towards the present Hadley green, whilst, to the left, commences a rather considerable depression to the north of Hadley church, from which depression there is once more a rise in the direction of the Common eastwards. Warwick would hardly have allowed this to lie in his immediate rear, though it might have served as a protection to the left flank of his line. If then we suppose that this wing rested upon it, or was drawn slightly in advance of it, we may easily conceive of the whole position as extending westwards, past Old Fold Farm, then a moated manor-house belonging to the Frowykes, which may have been within the line or behind it, to the point where the meadows touch the existing New Road. Somewhere here the right flank may have been posted, unless we can imagine it to have reached yet further to the west, and that, when it drove in Edward's left, the latter fell back through Barnet by way of Wood Street. In this case Oxford's troops, in returning to the field, might easily have been misled in the fog as to the quarter from which they had left it.

The nearly uniform elevation lends credibility to these suppositions. A level surface was in those days almost essential to the effectual movements of a heavy-armed horseman, whose war-steed, in addition to the mail-clad rider, was burdened with weighty defences of his own. The levels, however, throughout the area which has been indicated, present little variation. At the obelisk we find 417. 3,*—at the Hadley Post Office, 429. 9,—along the high road in front of Pimlico House, 430,—in the fields west of Old Fold, 419,—and at the New Road in the same direction, 397. North-west of Old Fold there is a rapid descent. In short, nowhere else do we find the fair plain, half a mile from Barnet, on the top of the hill upon which the town stands.

When Edward approached, he sent his troops forward through the town, permitting none to remain in it, and established a camp on its northern outskirts. For him it was a matter of moment that no engagement should take place before the next day. Unlike Warwick's army, which there is reason to suppose was already made up, and for which consequently an immediate encounter would have been more advantageous, his was receiving continual reinforcements, as one after another band joined his standard.† He accordingly issued orders that his encampment should be protected by palisades and trenches against a night attack, and bivouacked in the open field under arms. Edward possessed many of the instincts of an able general, and in his dispositions against the coming conflict seems to have been acutely impressed with a sense of the vast issues at stake.

As night drew on, a thick mist began to overspread the surrounding country, due, according to the superstitions of the age, to the incantations of Friar Bungay,‡ a sorcerer, of whom lord Lytton has made large use

* These are taken from the last Ordnance Survey.

† Grafton.

‡ Fabyan.

in his Last of the Barons. The deepening fog veiled the lustre of the Paschal moon and rendered the needful evolutions difficult of execution. It is said that, owing to the thickness of the weather, Edward was deceived as to the exact position of the enemy, and that a portion of his army missed, in consequence, the ground which it ought to have taken up and strayed to its right in the direction of Enfield Chace, overlapping thereby the left of the adversary. In this case it may have been drawn into the vicinity of Hadley church,—not the present edifice, which was not erected until some twenty, or more, years afterwards, and the tower of which was not completed earlier than the beginning of the following century. There had however been a church on the spot for several centuries, dependent on the great abbey of Walden in Essex, but most certainly the beacon played no part in the battle, and indeed does not date from any very remote period. As a result of the same error Warwick's right became prolonged beyond the left of the Yorkist army, instead of facing it. During the night his artillery, in which he is said to have been the stronger, had been playing from this part of his line upon what were believed to be the enemy's positions in front, but, from the cause just mentioned, the balls fell harmless, no enemy being within the range. It has likewise been asserted that, though the firing was sustained almost without intermission, it did little or no execution because, owing to the proximity of the rival hosts, the shot fell beyond the mark. Edward had taken the precaution of enjoining silence upon his soldiers, desirous, as has been stated, that the night should pass without disturbance, but in this was only partially successful. The tents we are told were so near together that "what for neighyng of horses, and talkynge of menne, none of both the hostes could that night take any rest or quietnes."* Thus the hours wore away upon that mist-enshrouded plain, over which the angel of death was hovering, until the darkness should be overpast.

The equinox was already passed and day was breaking about 4. With dawn the opposing leaders marshalled their hosts. Montagu, with the earl of Oxford, led the Lancastrian right, which was strong in horsemen. The duke of Somerset commanded the archers in the centre. Warwick in person and the duke of Exeter directed the left. The horse were stationed in either wing. Of these leaders the fidelity of the brothers Warwick and Montagu to the cause, in which they were embarked, was at least open to suspicion. Warwick had espoused it partly from resentment, and Montagu had been the personal friend of Edward. It was surmised that either of them would have made his peace rather than jeopardize his fortunes past recovery. Somerset, Exeter, and Oxford, on the other hand, were hereditary Lancastrians; the two former being connected by birth or marriage, or both, with the royal house. Edmund Beaufort, duke of Somerset, was a descendant of a legitimated son of John of Gaunt by Katharine Swynford, and nearly related, in consequence, to the Lancastrian princes. Henry Holland, duke of Exeter, was the great-grand-

* Halle.

son of Sir Thomas de Holland by Joan Plantagenet, the Fair Maid of Kent, who afterwards married the Black Prince and became the mother of Richard II. He had married Edward's sister Anne, the daughter of Richard duke of York, but she had procured a divorce from him. John de Vere, 13th earl of Oxford, was the son of John, the 12th earl, beheaded on Tower Hill in 1461, at the accession of Edward.

Edward, on his side, seems to have preferred a different formation, and to have massed his forces on three lines, the vanguard being commanded by Richard duke of Gloucester, his brother, who had just completed his eighteenth year. Edward himself conducted "the battle," or main body, in which the captive Henry VI was placed, and lord Hastings,* his chamberlain, who had landed at Ravenspur with his master, had charge of the rear. He had besides a company of fresh men, held in reserve, who, it is probable, in the sequel, determined the result of the conflict.

The armies being thus ordered, the respective chiefs harangued their followers. One of the chroniclers † professes to record the substance of their addresses, which may even have been reported to him by some who heard them spoken, though it is more conceivable

* Sir William de Hastings, cr by Edward IV, 26 July 1461, baron Hastings of Ashby de la Zouch. Executed 13 June 1483 by order of Richard III when Protector. "He was brought forth into the greene beside the chappell within the Tower, and his head laid upon a long log of timber, and there stricken off; and afterward his body with the head enterred at Windsor, beside the body of King Edward." Halle, quoting Sir Thomas More; Holinshed.

† Halle.

that, like the utterances of the Homeric heroes, they were put in the mouths of the speakers as the words which the exigencies of the moment rendered it natural that they would have pronounced. Warwick, according to this, encouraged his men with the assurance that they were fighting in the quarrel of a gentle and rightful sovereign against a tyrant, who had invaded the realm, "a cruell man and a torcious usurper," and anticipates that, in a cause so just, God must needs be their shield and defence. Edward, on the other hand, denounced his adversaries as traitors to the realm and spoilers of the poor commonalty. It was good policy on his part to represent himself as the promoter of the popular interests.

The trumpets now sounded and the onset began, as is generally understood, about 5 o'clock. At this hour the sun would have risen and was probably struggling fitfully through the mist. Archers on either side first discharged their arrows and the billmen* followed them into action. The battle would appear to have resolved itself into a succession of engagements or skirmishes over different parts of the field, not directed according to any fixed plan, a result easy to be understood, when the obscurity of the weather is taken into consideration. For a time the issue hung in the balance, and there was a period of the struggle when it seemed more than probable

* These bills were formidable weapons, much employed by infantry in the 14th and 15th centuries. They consisted of a broad blade fastened to a long staff, which blade had a cutting edge and was curved like a scythe, with a short pike at the back and another at the summit. They were used to dismount, wound, and dismember horsemen. Fairholt's Dict.

that victory would crown the efforts of the Lancastrians. Their right wing, under the leading of Montagu and Oxford, having outflanked the left of Edward's position, routed the troops in that quarter and drove them back in confusion through the little town of Barnet, and in the direction of Enfield Chace. So decided was the success of the moment, that certain of the fugitives carried the report of a Lancastrian victory to London.* Halle indeed maintains that they, who galloped thither with this intelligence, were lookers on and not combatants. Happily for Edward the fog concealed the discomfiture of the left wing from the rest of the army.

Now, however, occurred an unexpected incident, fraught with the most important consequences. Oxford's victorious soldiers had, it is said,† broken their ranks with a view to plunder, and, if this were so, their early success may have partly demoralized them. Rallied at length and returning to resume their places in the line of battle, they found themselves confronted with their own centre. The impetuosity of their movement, as we may imagine, had carried them necessarily out of their direct line. They had, so to speak, turned the enemy's flank. Re-issuing from the houses of Barnet upon the plain beyond, they were brought face to face with Somerset's archers, occupying the centre of the Lancastrian army. It was the custom of the age for royal and distinguished personages to adopt some particular badge or device, as a special

* John Rastell, The Pastime of People, A.D. 1529, ed. of 1811.

† Fabyan.

cognizance, and to have the same embroidered on the coats of their retainers before and behind, and occasionally upon the sleeve. These badges differed from crests, which were worn upon the helmet. Some of them, both in England and elsewhere, were so notorious as to have become absolutely identified with the individuals using them.* Louis XII was known by the porcupine; Francis I, as may still be seen in many a town and château of fair Touraine, by the salamander; Henry II, his son, by the interlaced crescents, in honour of Diane de Poitiers. Richard III of England adopted the white boar, Henry VII the portcullis, and so on. Lord Oxford's badge was a mullet, or star with five points, whilst King Edward's was a sun with streaming rays.† There was a certain amount of resemblance between these two badges, and the heavy fog hindered the difference from being recognised, except at close quarters. Accordingly, when Oxford, having wheeled round, was returning towards the centre of his own army, that centre, in which the archers were posted, supposing that the Yorkists were in full march upon them, poured a volley of arrows into the advancing troops. The air was filled with rumours and suspicion of treachery. A cry of treason was instantly raised, and Oxford's soldiers fled to the number of 800, their leader quitting the field at the same time.‡

* "Stanley did dream, the boar did rase his helm."—Rich. III. act iii. sc. 4.

† For the origin of this badge, see Henry VI. pt. III. act ii. sc 1. Conf. Halle, Holinshed.

‡ Stow

Here was the turning point of the battle. Edward now brought his reserve force into action, kept back for such a contingency, fresh and vigorous soldiers ready to act with effect wherever need might most require. Warwick, on the contrary, had to call upon men, already exhausted with their previous efforts, for renewed exertions, and the call was not responded to. The day was visibly lost, and nothing remained for him but to sell his life dearly. By 10 o'clock,* or at noon, according to some writers, victory rested with the Yorkists,† and Warwick and Montagu were slain. The commemorative obelisk, erected by Sir Jeremy Sambrooke ‡ in 1740, professes to mark the traditional spot where the great captain fell, and it is not unlikely to be correct, as somewhat to the rear of Warwick's

* "This battayle duryd fightynge and skirmishinge some tyme in one place and some tyme in an other ryght dowtefully because of the myste by the space of thre hours or it wer fully achivyd."—Harl. MS. 543, f. 31; Stow's Historical and other Collections. Stow says they fought in a thick mist from 4 to 10; ed. 1615. Halle, "from mornyng almoste to noone."

† "King Edward at length remained in possession of the field, through the aid of Almighty God and of the glorious martyr St. George." Harl. MS. 543, f. 31.

‡ Sir Jeremy Sambrooke acquired by purchase the estate of Gobions, otherwise Gubbins, and more anciently More Hall, the property of Sir Thomas More, in the parish of North Mimms, and to the left of the road leading from Potter's Bar to Hatfield. He succeeded his nephew, Sir Jeremiah Vanacker Sambrooke, of Bush Hill, Enfield (d. s. p. 5 July 1740) in the baronetcy, and himself d.s.p. 4 Oct. 1752 æt. 77, when the title became extinct. He was bur. in the churchyard of North Mimms, where his memorial still remains. Clutterbuck's Herts i. 452, 453, 466; Lysons ii. 271, iv. 2. Cf Gough's Camden i. 350, where the conjecture respecting Hadley church is obviously an error.

left. Salmon, who wrote his *History of Hertfordshire* early in the last century, says that "the place which the present Inhabitants take for the Field of Battle is a green Spot near *Kicks-End*, between the *St. Alban's* Road and the *Hatfield* Road, a little before they meet,"* and it is not altogether improbable that the scene would be identified by them with perhaps its most important episode. Warwick is reported to have dismounted from his horse by the advice of Montagu, who must have rejoined his brother after the dispersion of the right wing, and to have rushed into the thickest† of the fray, until he fell surrounded by foes. There is another tradition that, having previously dismounted, he leaped on a horse in the hope of escaping, but, coming to an impassable wood, became entangled in it and was killed. Montagu, at all events, lost his life in the endeavour to support his brother, thus atoning by devotion at the last for a fidelity previously questionable. Their dead bodies were placed on a cart and removed the same afternoon to London, whence, after exposure in coffins, "open visaged,"‡ at St. Paul's, for two or three days, that all men might be certified of their death, they were taken to Bisham Abbey in Berkshire and there interred.§

Somerset and Oxford quitted the field in all haste, with the intention of making for Scotland,|| but, fearing the risks of so long a journey, turned aside into Wales to Jasper, earl of Pembroke. The former was shortly afterwards beheaded in cold blood at the

* p. 56, ed. of 1728.

† Grafton.

‡ Grafton, Fabyan.

§ Weever, Funeral Monuments, p. 704.

|| Halle.

conclusion of the battle of Tewkesbury. Lord Oxford,* it is said, had previously parted from his company, upon discovering a design on the part of his chaplain to betray him,† and had made his way southwards. With certain companions, disguised as pilgrims,‡ he subsequently succeeded in making himself master of St. Michael's Mount, in Cornwall, where he was for some months besieged, and only surrendered the place upon obtaining favourable conditions. He afterwards passed several years abroad, where Scott makes him a prominent character in the charming romance of *Anne of Geierstein*, the historical inaccuracy of which almost goes beyond what is permissible. He survived until 1513, having led the archers of the vanguard in the army of Henry VII at Bosworth, and, though twice married,§ died without issue, being succeeded by his nephew. No later Lancastrian rising disturbed Edward's reign.

The duke of Exeter barely escaped with his life.‖ Fortunately for himself he was not personally so well known as most of the others, owing, it may be, to the circumstance of his having lived for some time in

* Such is the contradictory character of the relations, that we find it also stated that Oxford fled into the country, and in his flight fell into the company of certain northern men, fugitives like himself from the battle, and with them went northwards, and afterwards into Scotland. Harl. MS. 513, f. 31; Stow's Historical and other Collections. In the Parliament of Westminster, 12 Edw. IV, prorogued to 24 Edw. IV, John Veer, knt., erle of Oxford, of Wyvenho, co. Essex, was attainted for his service to Hen. VI at Barnet field and otherwise. This attainder was reversed in 1485.

† Fenn's Paston Letters, *Letter 312.*

‡ Richard Carew, Survey of Cornwall, p 155.

§ He married Margaret Nevile, sister of Warwick and Montagu.

‖ Harl. MS. 513, f. 31.

exile abroad. Dangerously wounded and left for dead on the field from 7 in the morning till 4 in the afternoon, he was brought to the house of one of his servants, near at hand, called Ruthland,* where he was tended by a surgeon, and afterwards conveyed in disguise to sanctuary at Westminster. As Rapin relates it, upon consciousness returning, he crawled to the nearest house and found means to be transported thence to London.

To Sir John Paston, in a letter † written to his mother from London on the 18 April, the Thursday after the battle, we owe the names of some of the leading men amongst the slain. "There are killed upon the field," he says, "half a mile from Barnet, on Easter day, the earl of Warwick, the marquis Montagu, Sir William Tyrell, Sir Lewis Johns, and divers other esquires of our country, Godmerston and Booth. And on the King Edward's party, the lord Cromwell, the lord Say, Sir Humphry Bourchier of our country, which is a sore moonyd (moaned) man here; and other people of both parties to the number of more than a thousand." The bodies of the more distinguished on both sides were taken away, and many of them interred in the church of the Austin Friars in the city.‡ In Westminster Abbey was buried Sir

* It is a little doubtful whether this were the servant's name or the designation of his dwelling.

† Fenn's Paston Letters, *Letter 311*.

‡ Weever deplores the desecration of their burial-places, and states that their bones, with those of many more, had been disinterred, and dwelling-houses raised in the place. The residue of the church, he goes on to note, had been given over to the use of the Dutch inhabitants of the city, "who in that kinde can hardly brook any reverend antiquitie." Funeral Monuments, 419.

Humphry Bourchier, lord Cromwell, son of the earl of Essex and first cousin * of Edward IV, on whose side he fell, as well as another Sir Humphry Bourchier, son and heir of lord Berners, who perished in the same cause.† Weever gives the Latin epitaph on his monument.

> Hic Pugil ecce iacens Bernet fera bella cupiscens,
> Certat ut Eacides, fit saucius undique miles,
> Ut cecidit vulnus, Mars porrigit arma cruore,
> Sparsim tincta rubent, dolor en lachrimabilis hora,
> Lumine nempe cadit, quo christus morte resurgit.
> Bourchier Humfridus, clara propagine dictus.
> Edwardi Regis qui tertius est vocitatus,
> John. Domini Berners proles, et parvulus hæres,
> Quartus et Edwardus belli tenet ecce triumphum,
> Quo perit Humfridus, ut Regis vernula verus
> Cyronomon (Cup-bearer) mense sponse Regis fuit iste,
> Elisabeth, sibi sic sua virtus crescit honore.
> Annis conspicuus quondam, charusque Britannis
> Hic fuit: Ut celis vivat deposcite votis.

The common soldiers, with some of the commanders,

* Henry Bourchier, earl of Essex, had mar. Isabel, daughter of Richard, earl of Cambridge, and sister of Richard, duke of York. Weever 482; Stow 171, ed. W. J. Thoms.

† His will was proved at Lambeth P.C.C. by Elizabeth, the relict, 18 June 1471 (Book Wattys 5). It is so brief, and is characterized by so much appearance of haste, as to warrant a conjecture that it may have been executed in haste on the eve of the battle. From expressions in a letter written by Sir John Paston to his brother John, 13 or 15 Sep. 1471, it might be surmised that there was some talk of a marriage between the latter and Sir Humphry Bourchier's widow. "I pray you send me word how ye do with my lady Elizabeth Bourchier; ye have a little chafed it, but I cannot tell how; send me word whether ye be in better hope or worse." Fenn's Paston Letters, *Letter 315*.

were buried on the field, half a mile from Barnet, but no tradition survives as to the exact spot. Stow informs us that a chapel was erected, by order of Edward, on the site and a priest appointed thereto to say mass for the souls of the slain.* In his time this chapel had become a dwelling-house, of which the top quarters yet remained. Speculation as to the locality is not likely to be solved. The description would notwithstanding point to the vicinity of Pimlico House on Hadley green, in the parish of South Mimms, the site, beyond a doubt, of some ancient building. Here as elsewhere the derivation of the name has aroused and puzzled enquiry. The Hadley register records "a travelling woman buried from the pimblycoe house" on 10 Feb. 1673, which seems to imply a lodging-house of some kind, inn or otherwise.†

The Paston letters supply a very interesting contribution to the history of the battle. Two of the family, Sir John Paston and his brother, who bore the same Christian name of John,—no unusual circumstance in that age,—were present on the Lancastrian side during the engagement, at which the latter was wounded. There is something that comes very home

* Stow p. 423; Cf. Weever p. 704, who adds, "as the doctrine went in those daies."

† Besides the well-known district extending from Chelsea to St. James's Park, which is not found under the appellation in any existing document prior to 1626, the name is also met with at Hoxton, where, at the present day, there is a Pimlico Walk. Ben Jonson mentions Pimlico, in connection with Hogsdon (Hoxton), in The Alchemist. Whether Pimlico were originally a person or a place is a matter of controversy still. Thornbury's Old and New London; Isaac Taylor's Words and Places p. 195.

to us in the evidence of letters, especially when of nearly even date with the events referred to. In that to his mother, Margaret Paston, of 18 April 1471, already alluded to, Sir John says,* "I recommend me to you, letting you to weet, that blessed be God, my brother John is alive and fareth well, and in no peril of death; nevertheless he is hurt with an arrow on his right arm beneath the elbow; and I have sent him a surgeon, which hath dressed him, and he telleth me that he trusteth that he shall be all whole within right short time. . . . . . Item, as for me, I am in good case blessed be God; and in no jeopardy of my life as me list myself; for I am at my liberty if need be." The letter concludes with some guarded expressions, implying that even now the writer did not look upon the cause as irrecoverably lost, and he mentions the rumour that Queen Margaret and her son had at last landed in the west country.† A letter is likewise extant from the wounded John Paston himself to his mother, dated from London on the 30 of the month.‡ He is fast recovering from his hurt, and says, "Modyr,

* Fenn's Paston Letters, *Letter 311*. Gairdner, iii. 3. "Blyssed be God, my brother John is a lyffe and farethe well, and in no perell of dethe. Never the lesse he is hurt with an arow on hys right arme, be nethe the elbow; and I have sent hym a serjon, whych hathe dressid hym, and he tellythe me that he trustythe that he schale be all hole with in ryght schort tyme . . . . . . Wretyn at London the thorysdaye in Estern weke."

† They in fact landed at Weymouth either on the 13 or 14 of April. Holinshed.

‡ John Paston of Gelston (Geldeston in Norfolk, where he sometimes resided,) to Margaret Paston. A.D. 1471, 30 Apr. Fenn's Paston Letters, *Letter 313*. Gairdner iii. 6.

I beseche you, and ye may spare eny money, that ye wyll do your almesse on me and send me some in as hasty wyse as is possybyll; for by my trowthe my leche crafte and fesyk, and rewardys to them that have kept me and condyt me to London, hathe coste me sythe Estern Day more than V^{li}, and now I have neythyr met, drynk, clothys, lechecraft nor money but up on borowyng." The words indicate that his escape from the field was not unattended with difficulty, but, notwithstanding the melancholy state of his affairs, he writes in high spirits as respects the prospects of his party, having heard probably of Margaret's landing.

Many of the fugitives and wounded sought concealment, according to tradition, at North Mimms and other neighbouring villages. To such as stood in need of no surgical aid the coverts of Enfield Chace would have offered abundant shelter near at hand. But the slaughter of that blood-stained field spread sorrow and mourning, we may be sure, throughout the length and breadth of the land. The chroniclers tell us that Warwick's broken host dispersed and fled in all directions. The loss we know fell heavily on the inferior ranks, to whom, on this occasion, contrary to his usual wont, Edward instructed his followers to give no quarter. Evidently his purpose now was to kill, not scotch, his foe. We accordingly hear little about prisoners. Halle* says that their number could not be certainly known. Of those who perished few names have indeed been preserved. In the church of

* Grafton reports the same.

the Grey Friars, London, were buried Thomas a Par and John Milwater, esquires to the duke of Gloucester,* and we find mention likewise of one Thomas Bodulgate, a Cornish gentleman of consideration, the owner of many manors.† Connected with a small brass in the south transept of Hadley church, the most ancient memorial within the building, there are grounds for supposing that Thomas, the son of John Grene and a nephew of the Philip and Margaret whose names are thereon recorded, was of the number of the slain.‡ Sir John Paston, in the letter to his mother, after enumerating the more important personages, naturally confines himself to a mention of sundry names with which she would be locally acquainted, and no doubt survivors from many another county could have furnished correspondents with a list of equally sad interest.

The conqueror immediately rode back to London. He did not wait to follow up his victory in person or even to superintend the operations of troops, whose business henceforward was the pursuit and destruction of the vanquished. Henry, whom he had brought with him to Barnet, in order to be prepared against any contingency that might arise, accompanied him in his return, "rydynge in a long gowne of blewe velvet."§ Not improbably it was the attire in which he had ridden through the London streets on the previous Thursday morning, when, at the news of Edward's

* Stow's Survey, p. 120, ed. W. J. Thoms; Stow's Annals, p. 423.

† Parliament, 13 Edw. IV, A.D. 1473.

‡ Harl. MS. 1551, f. 55b.

§ Rastell, Pastime of People.

approach, the citizens were exhorted to remain true to the cause of the Red Rose. Likely enough that the alteration in his circumstances affected him but little. In the mental condition to which he had become reduced he could never have been more, even on the throne, than a puppet in the hands of others.

On reaching London Edward once again, as on the day of his first arrival, presented himself at the rood of the north door of St. Paul's and there offered his standard and returned thanks.* Later, the same afternoon, he passed through the city with Henry by Cheapside to Westminster, whence the dethroned prince was sent to the Tower, never again to quit its precincts alive.† No tradition has reached us that the victor subjected his captive, during the course of this triumphant progress westwards,—for so it must be regarded,—to any unnecessarily contumelious treatment. He was probably instigated by a simple desire to bring the fact of his success distinctly home to the popular mind. The remark was current among the people that the expression of his countenance was not so joyous as might have been expected, after the overthrow of so dangerous an antagonist as Warwick, and this was attributed to sorrow on account of the death of Montagu, for whom, notwithstanding his recent opposition, he still entertained sentiments of genuine friendship.‡ It was mainly owing, as has been reported, to this cause, that he permitted the interment of the brothers in Bisham Abbey.

After making large allowance for the imperfect

* Fabyan, Grafton, Halle.

† Fabyan, Rastell.

‡ Halle, Grafton.

communications of that age, it is difficult to explain the discrepancy between the statements which have reached us, both as to the relative strength of the armies engaged and the number of the slain. Many of the historians were nearly contemporary with the events related, whilst others enjoyed facilities of information which ought to have insured some approximation to accuracy.* Rastell, for example, whose father-in-law, Sir John More, resided at Gobions, may have listened, on the spot, to many local traditions. Reinforcements were probably joining either army, that of Edward especially, up to the last moment; but this reflection is insufficient to remove the difficulty. The preponderating testimony seems, however, to assign the greater force to Edward. So say Halle and Grafton, and Rapin follows them. Philippe de Comines states that Clarence took over to his brother a body amounting to no less than 12,000 men—an admission leading indirectly to the same conclusion. The disciplined troops too, who accompanied Edward from the Continent, must have given him an advantage not to be measured only by their numerical strength, whilst the suspicions attaching to Montagu may have been a source of grave embarrassment to his brother. The Warkworth Chronicle, whose writer's sympathies were Lancastrian, and which was probably compiled about the year 1473, puts the number of Warwick's army at 20,000. That, on the other hand, which has

* Warkworth was Master of St. Peter's College, Cambridge, 1473-1498. Philippe de Comines died in 1511. The Chronicle of Robert Fabyan, a London alderman, was first printed in 1516. John Rastell died in 1536, Edward Halle in 1547.

certainty hanging over it. At Marston Moor or Naseby, and in recent times at Gravelotte or Sedan, one can picture to one's self by report every turn of the engagement, one knows where this or that renowned captain was posted, where the different arms were engaged, and where the most desperate or telling efforts were made and met. All this unfortunately is beyond our power here. At best we can only approximately fix the precise place of an encounter, between which and ourselves four centuries intervene. Those were not days in which generals made their reports to head quarters, or special correspondents, aided by pen and pencil, and under no obligation to use merely professional terms, sent home descriptions of what they had witnessed, so vivid, that fireside students can follow with the mind's eye every evolution of the hostile armies. This disadvantage we must perforce labour under, but we have at least contemporary testimony how the opposing forces met on the plain half a mile from Barnet, whilst other considerations guide us to a selection of the ground, which an experienced leader like Warwick might presumably have occupied. As to the more marked features of the battle the chroniclers, though differing so widely as to the number of the combatants and the extent of the slaughter, are in the main agreed.

To the writer of these pages, to whom the neighbourhood has been familiar from childhood, and without doubt to many others as well, there is a pleasure in recalling the successive events which have illustrated the scene where our lot is cast. Barnet has greatly changed from the little town, through which

Edward passed on his way to a battle upon which his throne depended, but, behind the plastered or brick-faced fronts of the buildings lining its modern street, are perhaps hidden the timbers of dwellings, from whose windows men and women and little children looked out upon the victor, as, early on that Easter afternoon, he rode past with Henry in his train. Or, strolling at our leisure through the pleasant meadows near Old Fold, from which the setting sun may be seen sloping to the west over the woods of Dyrham Park (anciently Durhams), as the eye ranges over a fair and far prospect in the direction of Elstree, we may muse upon the bloody scene for which the same meadows furnished a stage, when York and Lancaster "charged with all their chivalry" upon the plain encumbered with the dead bodies of kinsmen fallen on opposite sides in that unnatural civil strife. It would be interesting to know under what banner the inhabitants of Old Fold ranged themselves, and how it was occupied during the battle. We can hardly be mistaken in concluding that it fell within the Lancastrian lines, and, if so, could scarcely have failed to be affected by the shifting fortunes of the day. Did gallant soldiers issue from its gate to take their part in the fray? Did any wounded fugitive cross its moat, at the close of the engagement, to seek shelter or to die? Who can tell whether Warwick may not have established his head quarters within those moat-defended precincts? We are not likely to be informed, but there will be at least food for fancy in the surmise.

Two forms are chiefly present to the imagination on

the blood-stained field of Barnet, and two causes are identified with them. The forms are those of the two princes, in whose names and for the promotion of whose ostensible interests the contest was waged, and by the causes we understand not those of Yorkist and Lancastrian merely but those of advancing or retarded progress. The words progress and conservatism might have been substituted, had not the latter term been open to misconception. On the one hand, we have the meek and gentle figure of Henry, a crowned saint, of an almost feminine sensitiveness and delicacy of feeling, wholly unfitted by natural gifts for the place which he was born to fill in that turbulent age, even if occasional aberration of intellect had not interfered to put him at one time and another completely aside. Alone of the princes of his day was he capable of such renunciation as was contained in his answer to the offer of a large sum from Cardinal Beaufort's estate. "My uncle"—he replied—"was very dear to me, and did much kindness to me whilst he lived; the Lord reward him! But do ye with his goods as ye are bounden; I will not take them." There was a nobility of sentiment and grace of form in the refusal, which cannot fail of commanding admiration.

On the other hand, we see the fourth Edward, endowed with all those showy and external qualities of person and bearing, which were of a nature to sway the popular feelings, handsome, of gracious bearing, a stalwart typical Englishman, yet calculating, cruel, a voluptuary, and altogether unloveable, when the eye could penetrate beneath the surface. And, notwithstanding, he played a part, and a great one, in those events which have tended to shape the England of our own day and make it what it has become. With all his really beautiful characteristics, it may be a question whether, even if Henry's lot had fallen on peaceful times, the fifteenth would have known that national advance, silently germinating, whose outcome was reserved for the succeeding century. Underlying the contest between the Red and the White Rose, a struggle was going on between old ideas and new. Monasticism had served its purpose and was now become effete. Convent life was stagnant and corrupt. In earlier and ruder times it had played a useful, and indeed a very necessary, part. Art and letters, with all the civilizing influences attaching to them, found a home in the cloister, when the great world outside only rang with the sounds of actual or mimic warfare, but the desire for information was extending beyond convent walls. The foundations of Winchester and Eton responded to a craving, the consequences of which were doubtless little foreseen, nor in truth could have been. Added to which, the religious awakening referable to Wycliffe and the Lollards might have been hopelessly submerged at its birth, had not a strong undercurrent of healthy progressiveness carried it with the stream, to rise to the surface at a happier day. The merciless persecution of Lollardy, under the fourth and fifth Henrys, was, there is reason to think, conducted in an even more intolerant spirit than that which consigned Reformers to the stake, in the reign of Mary, and Popish recusants to the gibbet in that of Elizabeth. Closely connected moreover with the success of the House of York were the interests of the leading trading communities of London, and of the towns engaged in commerce. Edward made himself a favourite with the citizens, and he was the immediate patron of Caxton. The engraving, after Maclise's picture, of his visit with the Queen to the printer is well known. Simultaneously with these movements, the destruction of the ancient nobility, and consequent loosening of the feudal sympathies, during the wars of the Roses, led to the upgrowth of a new ascendant class, representative of enlarged ideas, of intellectual and material development, and of commercial activity. Lord Warwick may be contemplated in a sense, as lord Lytton has styled him, *The Last of the Barons*. But as the great nobles fell, the lesser gentry and the merchant class rose in consideration. The Reformation in the following century added a new stimulus to the spirit which was unfolding, and name after name rises to the recollection to testify of a generation conscious of a great inheritance, an inheritance which, after many vicissitudes lying between our age and theirs, has descended to ourselves as a priceless heirloom.

Pedigree to Illustrate the WARS OF THE ROSES.

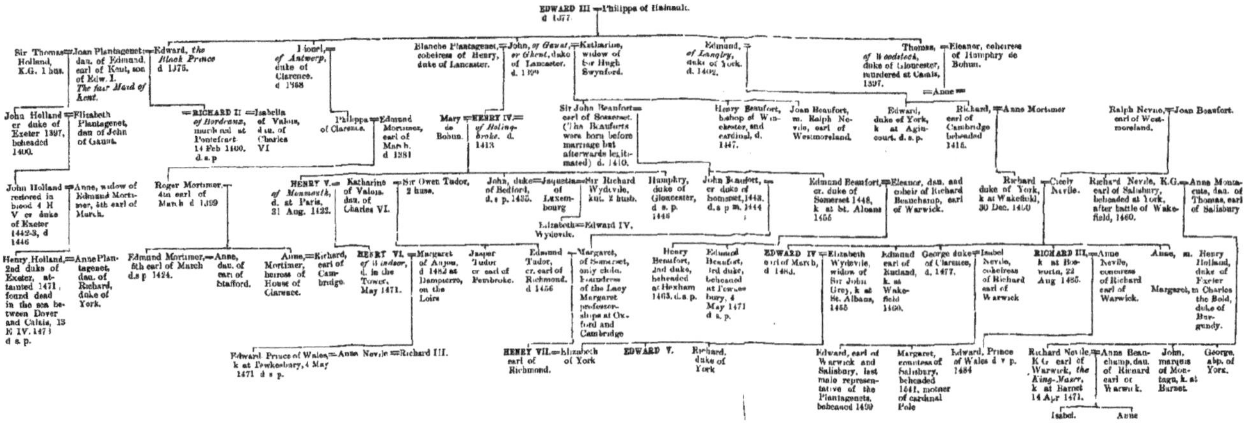

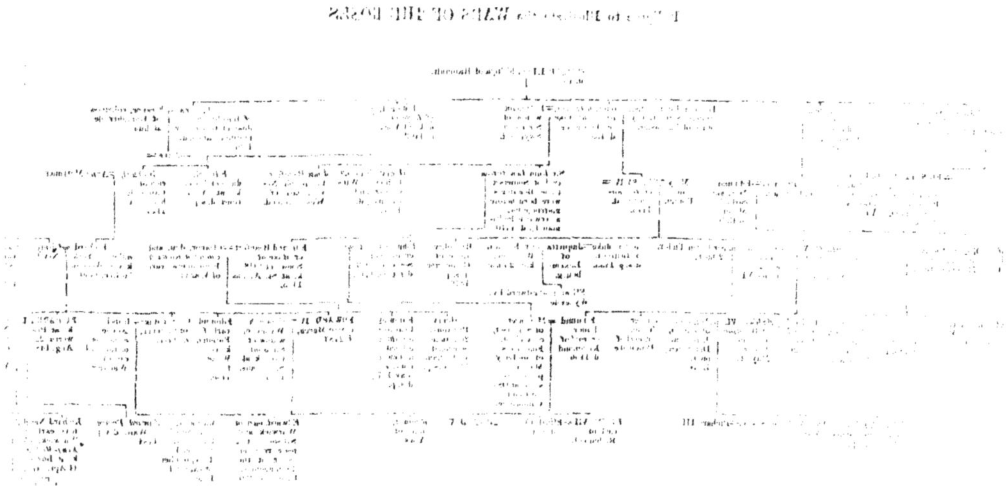

CPSIA information can be obtained at www.ICGtesting.com
Printed in the USA
LVOW03s1628050914

402660LV00018B/547/P

9 781241 555580